Boost Your Immunity:

Essential techniques for greatly boosting immune system strength.

Donald Bradley

Table of contents

Introduction

Your resistant structure is your fundamental gatekeeper instrument against intruders like microorganisms or diseases that can make you very wiped out.

It is fundamental to guarantee that you stay strong over the long run and placed all of the potential outcomes on your side to help your immune system. To do in that capacity, coming up next are five maneuvers to help you with making an effort not to be weakened with a cold or flu.

Chapter 1:
Good Nutrition

Eating healthy entails consuming a variety of fruits and vegetables and being hydrated. Enough to ensure you receive a variety of minerals and antioxidants that will assist your immune system to be strengthened. You should pay close attention to your consumption of selenium, vitamin E, and vitamin C in particular.

Fish and nuts, such as Brazil nuts, contain selenium. You may find vitamin E in spinach, seeds, and peanuts. Numerous vegetables, including broccoli, spinach, cauliflower, and sweet potatoes, contain vitamin C. When it comes to water, consuming a lot of it can assist your body remove toxins and germs that might make you sick.

These are some suggestions for your shopping list:

Fish

A great source of selenium is fish, particularly tuna. Selenium content in an ounce of tuna is about 30 mcg. One of the vital elements for human well-being and defense mechanisms is selenium, a strong antioxidant. For an adult, consuming 55 micrograms of selenium per day is advised.

Selenium content in other fish and seafood ranges from 12 to 20 mcg per ounce. Another great option for boosting the immune system is salmon. It has a significant amount of "good fat" (omega-3), which is believed to boost immunity and lower the risk of heart disease.

Lentils

Fish may be easily replaced with lentils if you follow a vegan or vegetarian diet. Around 6 mcg of selenium may be found in one cup of lentils. They are also a fantastic source of protein, fiber, and minerals that support the immune system.

Garlic

Another food, garlic, has similar effects on our immune systems to zinc. There is some evidence to support the claim that garlic helps stop the spread of viruses. According to particular research, even individuals with malignant growth had the choice to increase their intake of garlic in order to strengthen their immune systems.

Blueberries

Antioxidants are plentiful in berries as a whole. According to the number of antioxidants they contain, blueberries are the most abundant fruit and vegetable. Research has connected blueberries to a decreased risk of stomach obesity, cholesterol, heart illnesses, and cancer in addition to demonstrating the impact of blueberries on our immune system.

Sunflower Seeds

Vitamin E levels in sunflower seeds are quite high. 15 milligrams, or 76% of your daily need, may be found in one ounce. Like selenium, vitamin E is a strong antioxidant that aids in the immune system's ability to fight illness.

A diet high in zinc, selenium, vitamin E, and vitamin C will probably help you strengthen your immunity. Even while it's nice to consume a variety of therapeutic foods, it's not always feasible to provide our bodies with all the vitamins, minerals, and antioxidants they require to be healthy. Supplements are a fantastic choice at such a point.

Chapter 2:
Practice Great Cleanliness

The main stunt to not get influenza or a virus is to keep away from its antigens by rehearsing great cleanliness. That means to restrict, however much you can, your openness to infections or microbes.

The objective of the infection is to track down a host, a cell in the body. Our inborn invulnerable framework is the specialist on-call of our body, which incorporates our skin. Our skin, being the primary line of the guard, fills in as a surface hindrance to prevent infection or microbes from getting into our body.

That is the reason when we are in the influenza season, you see indications of cleaning up all over the place. By cleaning up, you obliterate the antigen before it hurts the body. You ought to clean up before each feast, after going to the restroom, or in the wake of contacting another person (like a handshake) or something out in the open. It is additionally fundamental to be aware of when you go after your face since the infection is bound to enter through your mouth.

Chapter 3:
Remain hydrated

Your body will be able to remove the toxins that might make you unwell by drinking enough water. Dehydration affects 75% of individuals regularly, which is probably one of the main reasons why the majority of us get sick or take longer to recover from diseases.

To remove poisons from our bodies, water is essential. We can't get rid of the poisons quickly enough if we don't drink enough water. Viral or bacterial toxins are both examples of toxins. Water consumption can help stave against illness. By carrying a bottle of water with you at all times that you can refill, you can start drinking more water. It is advised to drink two to three liters of water per day.

Chapter 4:
Establish a bedtime schedule

You must make sure that you receive enough sleep for your immune system to be operating at its best. It is advised to acquire seven to eight hours of sleep every night since it is vital to our immune system. The body can rejuvenate in that amount of time.

Getting enough sleep will improve the body's white blood cell defenses against disease and lessen cold and flu-related symptoms. Try to establish a nighttime schedule that enables you to receive the hours of sleep you need to have a decent night's sleep. Here are some suggestions to help you get better sleep.

- *Establish a Routine*

It has been demonstrated that a schedule will deceive your body into going to sleep at a particular hour. Try to be aware of your behavior. Do you ever get tired? If so, be careful to turn it in before that hour. Make a schedule that will enable you to do everything before that hour and retire to bed. You may also program an alarm to alert you when it's time to get ready for bed. You will be more effective in establishing a pattern and be less prone to forget what time it is if you do this. A good addition to your calendar is a sleep ritual. A decent sleep routine enables you to unwind, disengage from life's stress, and Slowly signal to your body that it's time to rest.

- *Create a Comfortable Environment*

It might be time to take a look at your bedroom and consider how you might create a more conducive environment for a restful night's sleep. Never undervalue the power of clean linens or how comfortable your bed and pillow are. You'll probably have trouble sleeping or staying asleep if you're uncomfortable. The temperature of the space and the degree of ambient noise are other factors that affect comfort. Try using a white noise machine or a fan to sleep. It could be easier to sustain your sleep if there is a consistent sound in the room. Try putting a dab of lavender essential oil on your pillow if you enjoy them; it will soothe the mind.

- *Don't Do This*

The two to three hours before going to bed, abstain from alcohol, smoking, spicy or acidic foods, caffeine, and heavy meals.

- *Consult a Specialist*

It could be a good idea to speak with your doctor or a sleep specialist if you've tried all those suggestions but are still having trouble falling asleep. They might offer you additional treatments as well to help you sleep better.

Chapter 5:
Take Control of Your Stress

Illnesses are significantly influenced by stress. One in three people reports feeling extremely stressed out in their daily lives, which raises the possibility of hazardous viruses already present in our bodies becoming active. Stress impairs our body's capacity to produce antibodies that can fight off foreign substances. Stressful events and everyday stress can be harmful to our immune systems. Your immune system will get stronger the more stress-reduction exercises you can incorporate into your daily routine. Here are two suggestions to help you lower your stress levels and strengthen your resistance to infections.

Change Your Mentality

By being more certain and present at the moment, you may change how you appear. According to research centers across the globe, positivism is a brand that promotes thriving and lessens the likelihood that you will become sickly and disabled. Not only are these people more active in their safe environment, but they also give off signals of being better overall.

All things considered, you have a choice in how you respond to whatever happens around you. Either a half-full or a half-empty glass is used to see it. Focusing on appreciation is a great way to start further boosting your mood. Finding things to be grateful for can help you see the best outcome in any situation. You can do this by noting in a diary the frequent gratitude you must express.

Develop mindfulness

You may take a fresh outlook on life by including a mindfulness practice to manage your stress.

Being mindful is being able to focus just on the here and now and stop thinking about the past or the future. A stronger immune system and less physical stress are both results of less mental stress. Take three deep breaths and try practicing mindfulness breathing.

- Taking a breath via your nose

- Using the mouth to exhale

Repetition twice more

Repeat this attentive breathing practice a couple more times during the day for a total of five mindfulness breathing exercises.

Take Advantage of Aromas' Power

Essential oil aromas can help you strengthen your immune system while calming the environment. Lavender oil is one of the most efficient essential oils. Antioxidants included in lavender, a potent oil, aid in the body's defense of its cells against poisons.

To assist eliminate allergens, add a fresh aroma to your house, and aid in relaxation, you may use it in a diffuser. To get better sleep, put a drop of lavender oil on your pillow.

Adding two to four drops of lavender oil to your bathwater is a wonderful additional usage for it. You can experience a profound sense of relaxation and assist your body to rid itself of pollutants by using lavender oil.

Anyone may focus on strengthening their immune system to improve their chances of remaining healthy during a bacterial infection or a flu season. As you have seen from this five-step plan, consuming particular foods and reducing stress can increase our chances of avoiding disease. Additionally, you have the chance to get more rest, which will aid the body in battling infections.

When you follow those five steps, you'll probably realize that you have more energy and can do more of the activities you enjoy when you're healthier. There are several benefits to maintaining good health!

Try to continue living this way all year if you can since it will strengthen your immune system's capacity to fend against pathogens. It not only increases your chances of being healthy but also hastens your recovery time if you do become unwell.

Chapter 6:
Exercise and immunity

Battling another cough or cold? Feeling tired all the time? You may feel better if you take a daily walk or follow a simple exercise routine a few times a week.

Information
Exercise helps decrease your chances of developing heart disease. It also keeps your bones healthy and strong.

We do not know exactly if or how exercise increases your immunity to certain illnesses. There are several theories. However, none of these theories have been proven. Some of these theories are:

Physical activity may help flush bacteria out of the lungs and airways. This may reduce your chance of getting a cold, flu, or other illness.
Exercise causes change in antibodies and white blood cells (WBC). WBCs are the body's immune system cells that fight disease. These antibodies

or WBCs circulate more rapidly, so they could detect illnesses earlier than they might have before.

However, no one knows whether these changes help prevent infections.
The brief rise in body temperature during and right after exercise may prevent bacteria from growing. This temperature rise may help the body fight infection better. (This is similar to what happens when you have a fever.)

Exercise slows down the release of stress hormones. Some stress increases the chance of illness. Lower stress hormones may protect against illness.

Exercise is good for you, but, you should not overdo it. People who already exercise should not exercise more just to increase their immunity. Heavy, long-term exercise (such as marathon running and intense gym training) could actually cause harm.

Studies have shown that people who follow a moderately energetic lifestyle, benefit most from starting (and sticking to) an exercise program. A moderate program can consist of:

- Bicycling with your children a few times a week
- Taking daily 20 to 30 minute walks
- Going to the gym every other day
- Playing golf regularly

Exercise makes you feel healthier and more energetic. It can help you feel better about yourself. So go ahead, take that aerobics class or go for that walk. You will feel better and healthier for it.

There is no strong evidence to prove that taking immune supplements along with exercising lowers the chance of illness or infections.

Chapter 7:
Immune system booster for kids

Your youngster's resistance is in a fast improvement stage and is tested by his current circumstance and kindergarten or school, so it is essential to guarantee he helps the right beginning through the right wholesome help.

While working appropriately, the safe framework is fit to battle illness, microorganisms, infections, organisms, and parasites. Kids are persistently presented to microorganisms and organisms, however, openness doesn't generally mean a youngster will become ill. A solid insusceptible framework upholds a kid's normal protection against infection. On the other hand, a kid with a debilitated resistant framework is helpless or more vulnerable to colds, influenza, and more serious diseases.

How might you assist your kid with building serious areas of strength for an invulnerable framework?

Small kids get colds regularly because their safe framework is as yet created. Be that as it may, there are steps you can take to assist with lessening their number of days off. Natural powerhouses of insusceptibility are:

- Sustenance
- Rest
- Work out
- Climate
- Sustenance

Great sustenance is fundamental to creating and keeping the insusceptible framework sound areas of strength for and. Dietary lack might be liable for ongoing invulnerable issues as it is simpler for microorganisms or infections to grab hold when significant supplements are absent. Basic supplements that invigorate major areas of strength for a framework incorporate nutrients A, C, E, iron, and prebiotics.

Rest

Lack of sleep can bring down your youngster's insusceptible framework; this will make him more powerless to being impacted by infections and microorganisms. Your kid's timetable can be occupied; most children shuffle sports and after-school exercises on top of school work. Kids must appreciate and learn through these exercises, but these should be offset with adequate measures of rest, which is basic to remain solid and sound.

Work out

Exercise can build a youngster's number of white platelets and lift white platelets' capacity to fend off diseases.

Chapter 8:
Techniques for supporting your energy if you are above 60 years

1. Get a flu vaccination

Having your yearly flu chance is one of the most remarkable approaches to defending yourself from this season's infection. This season's infection shot is shown to reduce the bet of hospitalizations in more settled adults by 40 percent and can diminish the general bet of flu illness by 40 to 60 percent.

The vaccination works by stimulating your protected structure to make antibodies. This shields against defilement.

There are different kinds of flu inoculations. A couple of inoculations are open to people, in light of everything.

Fluzone High-Part and Fluad Quadrivalent are unequivocally for adults ages 65 and more prepared.

Fluzone High-Piece. This vaccination contains on numerous occasions a bigger number of antigens than the standard inoculation. Your body makes more antibodies to fight this season's infection considering more huge degrees of antigens. People with the high-piece vaccination had 24% fewer flu sicknesses stood out from individuals who had a standard flu shot.
Fluad Quadrivalent. This vaccination has an extra fixing called MF59 adjuvant. This lifts the safe response and besides makes more antibodies to protect you from flu.

The occasional disease changes reliably. This suggests flu shot changes likewise established on expected contamination strains. To remain shielded, getting accessible vaccinations reliably is critical. You can have this season's infection opportunity from a specialist at your essential consideration doctor's office, a pharmacy, or a flu community in your space.

You can in like manner get some data about pneumococcal vaccinations to shield against pneumonia and meningitis.

2. Eat an enhancement thick eating routine

Eating a fair, supplement-rich eating routine is a huge technique for aiding your invulnerable structure. This integrates eating a ton of verdant food varieties, which contain enhancements and cell fortifications to propel incredible prosperity.

Different supplements and minerals expect a section in staying aware of the safe structure. The best method for resolving your issues is to eat different food sources.

Unequivocal enhancements that expect a section in safe prosperity include:

B supplements.

B supplements are found in dairy things, grains, meats, eggs, and beans. The absence of vitamin B12 is ordinary in more settled adults. Ask whether you truly need improvement.

L-ascorbic corrosive.

L-ascorbic corrosive is found in numerous food varieties developed starting from the earliest stage, red and orange sorts, and citrus natural items. A considerable number of individuals can get enough from food and by and large an improvement isn't needed.

Selenium.

Selenium is a malignant growth counteraction specialist that is found in unobtrusive amounts in various food sources. Sources consolidate nuts, meats, and grains.

Zinc.

Zinc is a mineral is found in shellfish, cheddar, beans, lentils, and meat. A large number of individuals can get enough from their eating routine anyway in phenomenal cases, an improvement may be recommended.

There is some evidence that a Mediterranean-style diet can maintain extraordinary immune capacity. A Mediterranean eating routine can similarly expect a section in helping with preventing and supervising steady diseases.

This particular eating routine integrates plenty of natural items, vegetables, whole grains, and beans. It similarly highlights strong fats from sources like fish, olive oil, olives, nuts, and seeds.

Hunger decreases safe capacity, which constructs the bet of affliction, according to a 2019 researchTrusted Source. If you are encountering trouble eating enough or getting an adequate arrangement, chat with your essential consideration doctor. You can similarly work with an enrolled dietitian if you need some extra help.

3. Keep on moving

It's basic to keep on moving as you age since activity enjoys many benefits. It can save solid areas for you versatile as you age. Practice furthermore augments the bloodstream and seriously influences the body.

Additionally, ordinary genuine work is connected with better safe capacity, as demonstrated by the 2020 researchTrusted Source. It's believed that being dynamic forms the body's ability to recognize damaging interlopers.

4. Direct strain

Consistent strain can influence the body, including cutting down your insusceptible response. Exactly when under tension, the body fabricates the improvement of a synthetic called cortisol.

Cortisol helps the body with overseeing disturbing conditions. It moreover confines explicit actual cycles that aren't major in an endurance situation. This integrates the safe structure.

Over an extended time, this confined ability of the invulnerable structure can make you more vulnerable to tainting.

It's trying to continue with an everyday presence that is completely freed from pressure, so sorting out some way to regulate pressure when it arises may be the most strong decision. A couple of decisions include:

saving a couple of moments for things that you track down lovely and loosening up, like scrutinizing or developing working out endeavoring care or thought approaches.
In case you're encountering trouble adjusting to pressure, ponder working with a subject matter expert.

5. Get a great deal of rest

Quality rest ends up being more huge with age. Getting adequate rest can additionally foster frontal cortex capacity, concentration, and memory.

Then again, the absence of rest can cause countless issues, for example, reducing the effectiveness of the rested Wellspring of the protected structure.

To deal with the idea of your rest, endeavor several these procedures:

☐ Guarantee your room is faint, quiet, and cool
keep a standard rest time routine at whatever point that is happening permits.

☐ Limit daytime rests to around 45 minutes avoid caffeine later in quite far alcohol, as it could dial backrest quality.

Expecting you are dealing with a dozing problem or various issues that keep you cognizant around nighttime, talk with your essential consideration doctor to check whether there could be any secret causes.

6. Support your stomach prosperity

Your body is home to trillions of minimal natural elements. Your microbiome is contained different accommodating minuscule organic entities, parasites, diseases, and protozoa. Most are found in the gastrointestinal framework (stomach) and accept various huge parts of your overall prosperity.

Your stomach is connected with your protected system. Right when your stomach microbiome is solid, your protected structure is better prepared to recognize and fight off pollution, according to a 2018 assessment.

The following are a couple of things you can do to keep a sound stomach microbiome:

Eat lots of fiber-rich food assortments, similar to vegetables, normal items, beans, whole grains, nuts, and seeds.

Endeavor developed food sources, for instance, kefir, yogurt, aged tea, tempeh, miso, kimchi, and sauerkraut conceivably utilize against microbial when significant

7. Quit smoking

The manufactured substances in cigarettes are known to hurt lung tissue and addition the bet of dangerous development. Smoking can in like manner cover your safe response, according to 2016 researchTrusted Source. People who smoke identity will undoubtedly have respiratory ailments, similar to flu, bronchitis, and pneumonia.

To additionally foster your safe system ability, ponder taking the necessary steps to stop or decrease smoking. There are many smoking ends help, for instance, nicotine patches or nicotine gum. Certain people moreover find the treatment or care bunches strong.

You can moreover consult with your essential consideration doctor about prescriptions to decrease cravings for cigarettes.

8. Contribute energy outside

Being outside enjoys such endless benefits for your prosperity. Numerous people put away that open door in nature helps with decreasing their tension. Another award of outdoor time is vitamin D from moderate sun transparency.

Vitamin D sustains the protected structure. Exactly when your vitamin D levels are adequate, they could help with preventing bothering and a couple of insusceptible framework contaminations.

A 2017 review by a trusted Source proposes vitamin D may moreover help with thwarting explicit pollution. Right when more than 11,000 people were analyzed, experts found that individuals who improved vitamin D had less respiratory pollution.

Past salmon and burger liver, there are moderately barely any food sources that are typically high in vitamin D. Dependent upon where you live, your complexion (melanin, or skin pigmentation, plays a sole in how much vitamin D mix that occurs from sun transparency), and how long you spend outside, it may be challenging to get adequate vitamin D from food and the sun.

If your vitamin D levels are low, your PCP could recommend an upgrade.